Impact Starts With Me

The Path of Self-Discovery

The Transition Chronicles

Dr. Ed Brenegar

The Transition Chronicles

An Imprint of Circle of Impact Press
Impact Starts With Me:
The Path To Self-Discovery

©2020 by Dr. Ed Brenegar
All Rights Reserved

ISBN (ebook): 978-1-7350656-1-8
ISBN (print): 978-1-7350656-6-3

No part of this book may be reproduced, stored in a retrieval system, or transmitted by any means without the written permission of the author and publisher.

Circle of Impact Press
Jackson Hole, Wyoming
Published in the United States

Table of Contents

Impact Starts With Me	7
Part One Understanding Who We Are	10
Part Two Believing in Yourself	14
Part Three A Circle of Impact Case Study in Self-Understanding	18
Part Four Impact Starts With Me	32

Impact Starts With Me

Liberation is happening. It didn't start with the COVID-19 pandemic but it is being accelerated by it. What is this liberation? People are asking questions about the changes that they are experiencing. They recognize that they are in transition. They are not sure why there is a change happening to them, but what they do know is that they are seeing things differently.

This sense of transition is personal. This is unusual and, oddly for them, freeing. It isn't primarily about how the world is changing. It is something inside of them. It is about how they are changing. Here are some examples.

There is a welder in Utah who asked his company to do more. They kept saying no. I said to him that sometimes we have to look beyond our work. We need to broaden our skills. I said, "Why don't you take some metal fabrication classes? Along with your welding skills, you could create metal sculptures." He liked that idea. He parted with a new perception of what is possible for him.

There is a corporate manager in North Carolina who realized that his team was not being given the respect due to them from the company. With clarity of insight, he had some ideas for strengthening his team.

There is a West coast executive assistant who realized that her sadness was a reflection of her love for the company that she served for three decades. The sadness came from a string of failures that jeopardized the company's standing in its industry. Through our brief conversation she realized that her love and sadness were shared by many in the company.

There is an East coast consultant who knew something was wrong with his company. After talking through the Circle of Impact model, he realized that the company is in a chaotic state of decline. It became clear to him that he was being set up as the scapegoat for the company's problems. With a clarity of awareness of his relationship with the company, he knew that it was time to leave the company.

There is a young professional from Nairobi, Kenya who asked if during a global crisis was it a good time to start a new business. I said, "Absolutely! When people are passively waiting for good times to return, it is also a good time to get ahead of everyone in planning for a new venture.

Each of these people's awareness of their lives changed in a matter of moments. Yet, the most significant change in self-understanding still waits.

Part One
Understanding Who We Are

There is a missing part of our lives. You can hear it in the way people talk about themselves. Many people talk about creating change. Others talk about living a meaningful life. Many people describe their lives by what they do.

Can you see the pattern here? The attitude is that our lives are like a bucket to be filled. What do we fill it with? Activities, labels, and connections to people for the purpose of feeling something positive about ourselves. Each of the persons above felt that they were in transition. The transition though was unclear. We've all been there. Some of us are there right now.

Change in Self-Perception

A sudden awareness came upon me two decades ago. While horseback riding with my family one July afternoon in 1999 in Jackson Hole, Wyoming, we rounded a bend on the trail and the magnificent vista of the Grand Tetons appeared in front of us. I heard a voice say to me, "It is time to stop talking about leadership, and lead."

At that moment, my self-perception changed. I knew that my life had to be different going forward. At that moment I knew that every time I was asked to take on a leadership role, I would do it.

We live in a consumer culture that promotes the idea that life's best should come to us. We are to receive good things because we are deserving. It is a "hand-out" mindset. The problem with this self-perception is that it does not take into account the billions of people who never receive life's best. It implies that they are undeserving.

There is something unanswered in this assumption. Precisely why we are deserving? What makes any of us more deserving than someone else? The problem is, at the very same moment that we are being made to feel deserving, we also feel guilty for it.

There are also many people who down deep inside themselves do not believe this to be true. They do not believe that they are deserving. They are not good enough, attractive enough, smart enough, rich enough, or powerful enough. This mindset creates anxiety and doubt. For some people, they plunge into activities of self-development intended to prove that they are worthy. Others turn the other way and hide from this inner conflict believing that they are not.

Can you see how we are manipulated into believing things about ourselves that cause not only inner turmoil, but also places us at odds with people around the world?

This is the transition point that most of us are facing today. It is about our self-awareness. How we perceive ourselves in the situations that we find ourselves in every day. Are we deserving of the good things that we receive? Do we understand why our lives are like this? It is like the cat chasing her tail. What do you do when you catch it and you discover who you are?

The stories I told above are just a few of the hundreds I could tell of people who had a change in perception about themselves and the places where they live and work. The stories fall into patterns of experience that many people share. While the transition that every person experiences is unique to them, there is ultimately one universal solution.

Like me, who heard a voice telling me to change, you too can learn to see yourself in a new way. The purpose of this book is about helping you see how to be a person of impact. When you see it and have a plan for creating impact, then you can say with confidence that "Impact Starts With Me."

Part Two
Believing in Yourself

When people recognize that they are in transition, it is not often clear to them. It is a different feeling than others they have felt before. It is a transition point that can have many sources. What they all share is a growing awareness of change that is leading them somewhere.

Here are two women whose stories illustrate this transition in self-awareness.

One woman, also from Utah, walked up to me as I was signing books at her local bookstore. She proceeded to tell me about the crushing blow that she felt when her husband abandoned her. He left for work one day and never returned. No phone call.

No letter. No email. Nothing. Four months later she discovered that he was in Nebraska. Now, two years after he left, she is standing before me in tears, telling me her story.

Can you see how if we need the external circumstances of our lives to be stable and predictable, just how fragile our lives could become?

After composing herself, we talked for a while, and I ended the conversation with this advice to her. "You are not the person you were when your husband left you. The person you are today is not the person you were two years ago. And the person you will be two years from today is not the person talking with me today."

She could not tell me what her transition meant. Only what it felt like. She was so fragile that she did not know what it meant to believe in herself. I encouraged her to read my book and then reach out to me when she was ready to talk some more.

Another woman I met in a bookstore outside of Denver. She shared with me how her family's life is very regimented. Her husband believes in order. She wanted me to know that she wasn't complaining. "It is just the way we are," she said. However, she told me that for some time she has wanted to do something totally on her own.

Can you see how if you've lived a very orderly existence that you can lose something about yourself? What is it that is lost? It is the part of you where creativity is an expression of your best self.

We talked about her renovating a house in Illinois that belonged to her mother's family. She'd do it by herself with support from her mother's kin. She wanted to break free, not in rebellion, but as a way to believe in herself.

Maybe it is the skills that I developed early in my career as a pastor that makes it easy for people to tell me these kinds of stories. Listening to their stories without judgment sends a message of belief.

Can you see that all it takes to begin to see yourself differently is someone taking the time to listen and affirm the transition that you are in?

There is a quiet liberation movement taking place that is not out of anger but out of belief.

Believing in yourself is not selfish. It is necessary, yet hard and a bit dangerous. Trying to believe in yourself without the right understanding can expose weaknesses in your life that can be hard to face.

Can you see how so many people hide from their true selves because they are afraid that self-understanding will prove that they are not worthy and deserving?

The goal of this transition is self-understanding leading you to a life of impact. It is important that YOU see that you can contribute to the world. It is not a contribution that someone demands of you, but one that is given freely. It is how we each become people of impact. To do so means that we can then say, "Impact Starts With Me."

Part Three
A Circle of Impact Case Study in Self-Understanding

It is very important that we think clearly about ourselves. The decisions that we make every day, not only impact our own lives but the lives of others. Being able to clarify our self-understanding is the beginning of changing our lives. For those who believe that you want to change the world, you must begin by changing yourself. We first begin with our self-awareness followed by establishing a purpose for impact that guides our life going forward.

In this section, I'm going to take you through the steps needed to accomplish those two goals. I call this a case study because every person is different. Your story is different. Your goals are different. And your purpose for impact is different. But creating a case study for yourself, you have a way of distinguishing yourself from others in a way that provides personal strength and focus for how you live each day.

The Circle of Impact Case Study method is like collecting pieces to construct a story. As we venture along this path, your perspective will change. You will become clearer about what you want for your life.

Let's begin with a description of the Circle of Impact

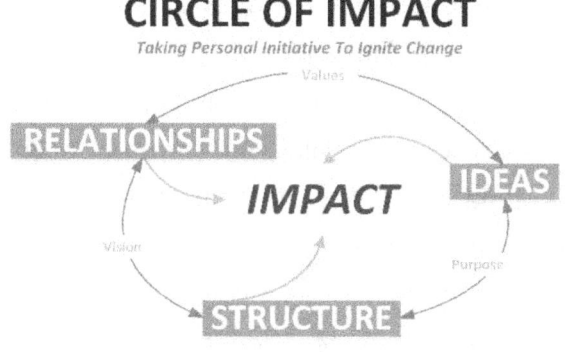

We all live at the intersection of three dimensions of our lives. These are the dimensions of Ideas, Relationships, and Structure. Through our ideas, we seek clarity, simplicity, and focus. In our relationships, we seek mutual respect, trust, and accountability. The Structure of our lives is divided between the organizations where we live and work and the social environment of those. In these structures we seek them to be pathways to impact. If we lack clarity, respect, trust, accountability and a pathway to impact in our lives, then we need to know why and how to change things so that we can live a life of impact.

The Ideas Dimension

There are four types of ideas in this dimension. Values are the foundation for the understanding of our Purpose, Vision, and Impact. Purpose and Vision are how our Values go beyond being mere ideas. Impact is the Focal Point for our Values having an effect in the world.

I want to be clear here. The Ideas dimension is not about having ideas that we carry around as kind of symbols of identity. They are not labels to define ourselves. Instead they are to clarify the kind of person that we desire to be.

Can you see that the purpose of the Ideas dimension is to lead to action through our Relationships in the social and organizational Structures of our life and work?

I call them The Four Connecting Ideas. They are like the muscles, ligaments, and tendons that provide linkage and strength to our self-understanding to be alive in the world.

Our values inform what our purpose for impact is. This leads us to the kind of structure we need to create the impact.

Our values also inform the kind of relationships we want.

When we share common values in our relationships we can create a shared vision for the kind of structure we need to create the impact we desire.

Can you see how our values are the foundation of understanding of every aspect of our lives?

Values ➡ Purpose ➡ Impact ➡ **Structure**

Values ➡ **Relationships** ➡ Vision ➡ **Structure** ➡ Impact

If we are unclear about our values, then we will be unclear about our purpose, and the meaning of our lives. When we lack clarity about our values and purpose, then we seek out safety in structures that ask little from us.

Since this is an exercise to create a clear self-perception, answer these two questions:

What are three values that are important to you?

What is one thing that you would like to change in your life or in the world?

Understand that this is just an exercise in learning how to approach these ideas. You can change what you think as often as you need to in order to gain the clarity that you need.

Now ask the third question.

Of the values listed, which ones directly relates to the change you'd like to create?

It is okay that not all of your values connect to your purpose.

My Values	→	
		My Purpose for Impact* is a...
		*A change that makes a difference that matters.

Use this table to help you visualize how to connect your values to your purpose.

What is it that truly matters to you? What idea or person or situation are you willing to invest in or sacrifice for that gives meaning and purpose for your life? This is where we discover a foundation of understanding for who we are.

Our values as ideas need to be acted upon for them to be fully understood. This is why impact is the focal point of the Ideas dimension. When we become clear about the impact of our values, then we have established direction and self-understanding.

Can you see now that Values are the Foundation of and Impact is the Focal Point of our Self-Understanding?

The Relationship Dimension

Our relationships take many forms. Some are family and friends, others are co-workers, employers, clients, and social media connections. Each relationship is different based upon the context and the purpose of it. However, for a relationship to function well it requires mutual respect, trust, and accountability. I say this because over the years, where I have found problems related to relationships, whether in families, the workplace, or the nation at large, the fundamental problem always seems to be a lack of respect, trust, and, where appropriate, mutual accountability.

Can you see how our relationships are dependent upon a strong values system?

Who do you have this kind of relationship? Create a list of either individuals or groups of people that you are regular interaction. For each relationship, mark Yes or No whether respect, trust, or accountability are strengths in the relationship.

My Relationships	Respect	Trust	Accountability

You can perform the same analysis by replacing those three values with ones that are important to you. In doing so, you are identifying those people with whom you could establish a relationship of shared purpose to create impact. If respect is missing, then the capacity for the relationship to have mutual accountability is probably low.

The purpose of this exercise is to demonstrate the importance of establishing your own standards for your relationships. If you are in a transitional phase in your life, it is important to surround yourself with people you can trust to be there for you as you experience change.

Why do our relationships matter? They matter because virtually everything we do and seek to achieve in life is dependent, in some way, on the assistance of others. Unless you choose to live off the grid as a hermit, you need people. And people need you. We need each other. The problem in many cases is that we don't have a clear understanding of how to live and work with one another.

In my book, All Crises Are Local, I make a distinction between family relationships and corporate ones.

> *A family is committed to one another through what we could call a promise agreement. The promise is to be faithful, caring, and attentive to each members' needs and desires. In this type of relationship, there is an assumption that the social structure of the family exists for the benefit of each member.*
>
> *A corporate relationship is a contractual one. The primary relationship is to the corporate structure. Each employee has a relationship of responsibility and accountability to the management structure of the company.*

This difference is rarely noted. Yet, it is a significant difference because the two relationships are based upon different sets of values.

Can you see how the difference between personal relationships and corporate relationships causes us to be divided people in our lives?

Fortunately, we do not want to live such fragmented lives. We do not want to be one person at home and a different person at work. We want to be a whole, complete person in all the situations we encounter. In All Crises Are Local, I describe this reality.

> *If an organization only operated according to contractual relationships, then each individual would truly be just a cog in a machine. But we know that this isn't true. We are not machine parts, but human beings. To be a human being is to be in relationship with other human beings. When our relationships are marked by respect, trust, and mutual accountability, we are on the way to seeing how love is the impact that we seek in all our endeavors.*
>
> *In an institutional setting, the quality of the culture is not determined by contract, but the degree in which we are able to establish relationships of respect, trust, and mu-*

tual accountability. These are the marks of quality in relationships.

Our self-understanding is not about us as an individual in isolation. It is about who we are and who we want to be in the context of our relationships. The higher quality of relationships that we have, the greater opportunity we have to create the impact that we desire.

Can you see how through our relationships we discover how to be whole persons of impact?

The Structure Dimension

The Circle of Impact model sees that organizational structures are not an end in themselves. They exist to serve an idea. Too often a structure will swallow up the idea with a loss of clarity of a purpose. This is why values are foundational and impact is the focal point for organizations.

Our challenge is that we are so surrounded by structures that it is difficult to see them for what they are. It is like fish trying to describe water. It is so all-encompassing that we cannot separate ourselves from it enough to be able to see it clearly. Yet, this is what we must do if we desire to create an impact that makes a difference that matters.

A basic starting point to understanding structures is to see that there are four aspects to every organization. There are products, programs, or services that are offered to the world. There are supporting operations that make it possible to sell and deliver those products. And there are the finance and governance functions which ensure sustainability and integrity. Every organization incorporates these four aspects in differing ways.

Structures are not just organizational ones. They are also orderly processes for accomplishing goals. You may need an organizational structure to achieve your purpose. Or not. The point is to first be clear about the impact that you want to achieve, and then go establish the structure you need. To be clear about your impact means that you have thought through the dynamics of the process for achieving your impact.

To create an impact-focused structure simplifies the kind of structure you need. Understanding the impact you want to create is to understand something that is singularly focused. The process may require many components. The focus is on the one change that you want to create. The process of creating a structure for impact is also a process of continued clarification of what your impact is to be. It is a constant learning process that is reflected in how you are changing your structure to fulfill your vision for impact.

Structures are an environment where people who have a shared purpose for impact, work together to achieve it. The four aspects of an organization will factor into how they establish the orderly process leading to impact.

Can you see how structures need to be established on a foundation of values with a purpose for impact as the focal point for the four aspects of an organizational structure?

Part Four
Impact Starts With Me

A Journey of Learning

Once you determine that you are going to create impact rather than to be impacted by circumstances, you have entered on a journey of learning. It is a journey with no final destination. It is a journey of impact that continues for the rest of your life. Think of it as a journey that takes you from place to place, and the next place is determined by the impact that you have had where you are right now. It is a journey of always being present with the people and places where you are right now.

This is the opposite experience than we have all had sheltering-in-place. We are not waiting. We are doing. We are not wondering. We are imagining. We are not consuming. We are creating. This is the change in self-perception that comes upon us when we decide that we want to live a life of impact, rather than what we have been doing.

What drives this change in self-understanding?

First is the belief that you have something to contribute. To contribute you must participate. To participate means that you will be doing things that you were not doing before. You are not waiting to be asked to participate. You are taking initiative to become involved in activities that represent the impact you want to create.

Second is that your meaning in life is found in the impact itself, not in the idea of the impact.

This second driver of awareness is the solution to a significant problem that affects every one of us. Turn on your television or open up your smartphone to any social media platform and what do you find? People who are paid to talk, to express opinions, and in many ways, to nullify human initiative. If you spend an hour or more a day staring at a screen absorbing the opinions of others, you'll never realize that those people are not contributors. They are not persons of impact. They will tell you that they are persons of influence. However, influence in our day means less and less because it cannot be measured like impact can be.

When you begin to do things that actually change people's lives for the better, you'll understand just how trapped you were in a simulated world of opinion, and not of action.

What Real Impact Looks Like

Recently, I have begun to do leadership training in Africa. I am working with a program that trains people in rural economic development. They begin with one chicken and build an agricultural enterprise that supports their families. The people that I am training help others to establish their own farms. A Kenyan couple that I trained have helped over 700 farms to be established. That is 700 poor families who don't have to beg, borrow, or steal to find money to feed their families and pay their children's school fees. There are others just like them in countries all over

Africa who are having an impact that is changing the rural communities of Africa.

When you decide to be a person of impact, you just start doing it. You start small and simple. It is a learning process. We have to unlearn the thinking that values opinion over impact. It is possible for you to have an impact by expressing your opinions. It is much more difficult because we have been programmed not to respond in action, but by reacting either by granting approval or rejection.

If you desire to create impact and don't know where to start, it is okay to say so. As the saying goes, "You eat an elephant one bite at a time." Creating a life of impact is a big deal that is accomplished one moment of impact at a time. It is okay to start small. It is the only way to learn. The place to begin is to return to the process of discovery using the three dimensions of leadership.

Solving a Problem

We begin by stating the question of our self-understanding as a problem.

> *I don't know what impact that I want to create.*

Is this an Idea, a Relationship, or a Structure problem?

> *It is a problem of a lack of clarity, so it is an Idea problem.*

The Circle of Impact problem-solving method is founded upon the principle that the solution to the problem is not in the problem itself. After deciding which dimension is the source of the problem, the other two dimensions become the sources of the solution.

> *If we are not clear about the impact that we want to have, then we need to create a structure - a process - that enables us to enter into conversations with people we know and respect to find out what kind of impact I can create.*

Out of these conversations some opportunity will emerge that provides you an opportunity to do something that makes a difference that matters. It is where we all start.

Your journey towards impact has begun. However, where you begin does not tell you where you'll end up. Let my friend Natalie's story illustrate how.

Natalie's Journey

Natalie worked for me as a virtual assistant during the time that I was writing my book, Circle of Impact: Taking Personal Initiative To Ignite Change. Late in that process I left the country for a month to attend a leadership conference in Vienna, Austria. I asked Natalie to read the manuscript while I was gone in order to tell me what she thought.

A few weeks after I returned she told me that the book had helped her realize that she needed to make a change in her life. Her purpose was not to be a virtual assistant but to help people reach their potential. She was currently involved in a project at her church where a group of women were preparing to go to Nicaragua to conduct a leadership conference for women there. Natalie was a keynote speaker for the group. She had a vision of working with women to develop their leadership potential.

A few months later her husband, Brian, retired, and they moved back to their hometown. Her vision was to return to their former church and create a program like the one they had been involved in previously. However, there was not an opportunity open for her to do that. Her purpose was the same, but the situation where she wanted to create impact was not.

Natalie and Brian are competitive ballroom dancers. As they became more involved with that world, she saw ways that she could build relationships there to encourage people to reach for their potential. A new opportunity within the ballroom dancing world arose with the opportunity to buy and operate their own dance studio.

Natalie's journey is still unfolding, but her purpose is the same. She and her husband have now a business structure that provides them a basis for long-lasting relationships with their teachers and customers. Could they have seen that this is where they would be two years ago? I don't believe so. However, when we organize our lives for impact, the focus remains the same, while the actions may change.

Believing that "Impact Starts With Me"

Remember my story of hearing a voice tell me, "It is time to stop talking about leadership, and lead." At that point in my career I had been deeply involved in the world of leadership for over 15 years. I had established a collegiate leadership program, started a leadership consulting business, and had earned a doctorate in leadership ethics. Those achievements were not destinations, but places of learning along the path of my journey.

On your journey, you can only be where you are right now. It does no good to raise your expectations beyond what is realistic for this moment in time. Think instead, what is the contribution that I can make right now that makes a difference that matters? When you take this mindset, then you are seeing how "Impact Starts With Me" right now. There is no waiting for the right time to come. It is right now.

There are two things to remember about this journey.

It begins with your self-understanding of believing that you can be a person of impact. This is not about you becoming someone else. It is about you discovering within yourself the qualities and capacities to make a difference that you can see as an impact that makes a difference that matters.

I cannot overemphasize the importance of your self-perception being one of belief, affirmation, kindness, and patience with yourself. If you have had doubts about yourself, or you have been afraid to take some action because it felt risky, please understand that what held you back in those moments was you not understanding what you have to contribute to the world. There is no universal measure that applies to everyone in the same way. You are the measure of your own values and sense of purpose for impact.

The other thing to remember is that the more you create impact, the more your perception of the world will change. It will impact your relationships.

Many people who live by the opinions of others will not understand. Yet, quite possibly they may see something in you that inspires them to reflect upon their own lives.

So, think of this little phrase, "Impact Starts With Me", as the motivation to get up every day and find ways to be a person of impact. I can tell you from my own experience that our lives become full and rich in seeing our contributions touch lives and communities in beautiful ways.

May your journey of impact begin now. And if you would be willing, please share with me your experience and what you are learning. You can reach me at ed@edbrenegar.com. If you do so, I can tell you that it will impact me in ways that help others as well.

What are The Transition Chronicles?

We all live in a time of transition. It is different than just recognizing that change is happening. It is seeing that transition is a process along a path of change. The more we embrace the transitions that we are in, the more we can thrive in a time of uncertainty. The Transition Chronicles is an ongoing series of short books (5,000 to 12,000 words in length) that focus on various aspects of the transitions that we experience through the three dimensions of the Circle of Impact. All the Chronicles will first be made available as Amazon Kindle downloads. Later, softcover versions will be made available.

For more information about the series, even suggesting a topic for me to consider, you can contact me at ed@edbrenegar.com. Please either put the title of the short book or the series in the subject heading.

Who is Dr. Ed Brenegar?

Dr. Ed Brenegar is a global thought leader, coach, trainer and speaker. His purpose is to inspire and equip people world-wide to take personal initiative to create impact in their local communities. He provides training and coaching for people to assist their organizations and their communities to become leader-rich places of impact. He is the author of Circle of Impact: Taking Personal Initiative To Ignite Change. He lives in Jackson Hole, Wyoming.

Contact Information:

Circle of Impact Leadership: https://edbrenegar.com

YouTube channel - https://www.youtube.com/channel/UCturARDH_7uaLOnNRG9-G-A

ed@edbrenegar.com

+1-828-275-1803